PHOTOSHOP

ELEMENTS 2025

Guidebook

A Step-by-Step user guide for Novices and Professionals

Joseph Paul

Table of Contents

Table of Contents

CHAPTER ONE

Getting Started with Photoshop Elements

Introduction to Photoshop Elements 2025

Photoshop Components 2025 proceeds Adobe's long history of giving photo-editing programs for casual clients and specialists. Combining effective AI, rearranged workflows and modern imaginative devices in a proficient easy-to-use stage for picture altering and plan, the most recent form conveys a solid combo of highlights.

1. AI-Powered Features

Photoshop Elements 2025 uses Adobe Sensei, the company's AI engine, to perform many complicated editing tasks:

Object Removal — New Remove Tool automatically takes care of removing unwanted objects and elements from images, requiring very little human intervention to use.

Depth Blur — Makes your photos come alive with the depth of field effect that professional camera uses.

Color Swapping: Users can quickly swap colors of objects, although this still relies on selection tools versus AI-based segmentation

1. Guided Edits

Guided Edits are a staple of Photoshop Elements since they provide step-by-step instructions for creating professional looking effects and projects. As of 2025, there are a total of 59 Guided Edits that exist in all these areas:

Animated Effects: Give the dynamic look inside a static image.

Cinematograph Creations: Combine still photos and an animated effect

Makeup on Art: Add sparkles, textures, or color gradients to embellish images

2. Enhanced Creative Tools

This software adds a whole bunch of new and improved creative tools:

Quick Actions — A feature that enables adding animation/visual effects on the top of a photo with just one click.

Photo Merger: A feature for up-to-date modern backgrounds, merging photo objects or layers into composite images.

Collage Maker Updated templates and design options for social media posts or printable projects

3. Expanded Accessibility

Web and Mobile (Beta): Photoshop on the web and mobile apps (both in beta) for basic edits, background replacement, overlays This brings the versatility of Elements beyond just desktop users, perfect for editing on-the-go

Non-Destructive Editing: Instant Fix and Adjustments let you modify photos without overwriting the original image so that.

4. **Organized Improvements**: The Asset Manager has been introduced to help users manage information   efficiently.
   • Tag and Sort: Use AI-powered tags to organize your photos by people, places, or

events.

• RAW Support: Although limited, RAW file support is available after installing Adobe Camera Raw. However, compared to Lightroom, the features are basic.

5. Pricing and Licensing: Photoshop Elements 2025 costs $99.99, and an optional bundle that includes Elements Essentials costs $149.99. The license model is available for three years with no subscription fee, which is cheaper compared to Adobe's Creative Cloud plans.

6. Intended Users

Photoshop Elements 2025 is intended for a variety of users: new user who demands easy to use picture editor software; enthusiast who finds pleasure in activities including photo touching such as photo album, photo gifts and many more; and user who desires an affordable software package that offers the power of an editor. Still, this software targets fresh users and experienced editors but can be useful for beginners mainly due to its interface. Due to its variety of the options it has impressive reputation among other applications for photo editing.

System Requirements

Windows

• Processor: Any computer with an Intel 6th Generation or later processor or an AMD equivalent processor that supports SSE4.2 instruction set.

• Operating System: Windows 10 (Version 22H2) or Windows 11 (Version 23H2) 64-bit only; Windows 7 and Windows 8.1 download not supported.

• Memory: At least 8 GB of RAM.

• Storage: This version requires at least 10 GB of Windows partition free disk space for installing (additional disk space is required on behalf of downloaded content and temporary files).

• Display: Nova launcher with screen resolution 1280 x 800 with 100% scaling.

• Graphics: The hardware must therefore be graphical enabled that is, a graphics card that supports DirectX 12.

• Internet: Required for paving the way for activation of the product and receiving regular updates.

MacOS

• Processor: A better result will be achieved with Intel 6th Generation or a later generation of a device with an Intel core processor; Apple M1 chip or later.

• Operating System: macOS 13 or macOS 14 (macOS 14.4 or later release).

• Memory: At least 8 GB of RAM.

• Storage: Minimum system requirements required hard disk space for installation of at least 10 GB additional space for content downloads and temporary files.

• Display: Then in terms of display settings I preferred screen resolution of 1280 x 800 with 100% scaling.

• Internet: Provided to the company for purposes of starting the product and receiving updates.

Since the two systems must be compatible, both systems have to be 64-bit. The three benchmarks are faster with at least 4 GB of VRAM for the GPU and faster SSDs for more complex tasks.

Installation and Setup

To urge Photoshop Components 2025 on your computer, do these things:

Step 1: Get the Installer

1. Tap on the site interface to go to the Adobe Photoshop Components page.

2. To proceed with the application, you have got to sign in together with your Adobe ID; in case you do not have an ID, make one.

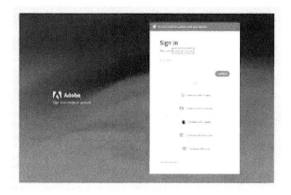

3. Find where to download Photoshop components 2025 and how to select the right variation for your working framework (Windows or Mac OS). Step 2: Get Your Computer Prepared

1. Guarantee you have got sufficient capacity on your computer to run it well, for more details check beneath the framework necessities.

2. The space prerequisite of the records on your computer ought to not be less than 10 GB. 3. Be beyond any doubt simply having got to the World Wide Web to download the installer, and check your permit on as well.

Step 3: Put Photoshop Components on Your Computer

1. Open the record you downloaded:

- For Windows: Double-click the .exe record.
- For macOS: Open the Terminal by squeezing the Cmd + Spacebar keys and sort terminal; Press return or enter; Twofold press the. dmg record and after that drag the app to your applications envelope.
2. Take after the steps on the screen:
- Agree to the terms. Choose where to put it with the help of imply which is found by default most of the time.

Interface Overview

Like other graphic designing tools, the user interface of Photoshop Elements 2025 has been developed in a very simple manner that anyone can use it easily. Below are the primary components of the interface:

1. Home Screen

•	Welcome Panel: A home page that has icons leading to Guided Edits, Quick Eds, and Advanced Edits.

•	Recent Files: Contains such options as Recent projects where projects are shown after the recent editing MIS.

•	Auto-Creations: Demonstrates how AI can create photo montage or a slide show.

2.	**Main Workspace**

Photoshop Elements offers three main workspaces, each tailored for specific tasks:

1.   Quick Mode: Simplifies editing with easy-to-use tools and automatic fixes.

o   Tools like crop, rotate, and red-eye removal are prominently displayed.

2.   Guided Mode: It offers lessons on creative effects and edits in a form of a sequence of lessons.

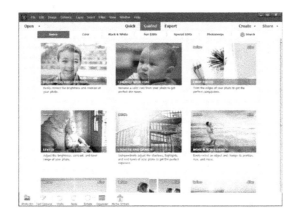

3.   Expert Mode: Has features advanced enough to be used for further refine of jobs as in Adobe Photoshop.

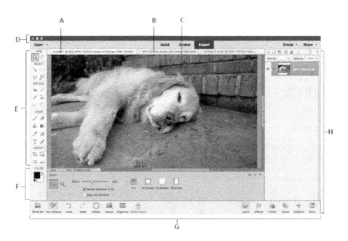

• Located on the left it contains features of selection, paint, crop, and adjust for image touch up among others.

• Every tool has specified its options at the top depending on the context that has selected which involves brush sensitive options like size, and opacity.

• Located on the right side of the screen, this panel will help the user control layers, masks and effects.• Thumbnails of layers can help best understand how the picture would look like.

• Located at the lowest level, it provides actions in a tool bar or fly out such as undo/redo, zoom and navigation.

• It can be launched by a button at the bottom of the screen and synchronizes with the Elements Organizer to view and handle files.

3. Toolbar

• Located on the left side, it includes essential tools for selection, painting, cropping, and retouching.

- Each tool opens context-sensitive options at the top, such as brush size and opacity.

4. Layers Panel

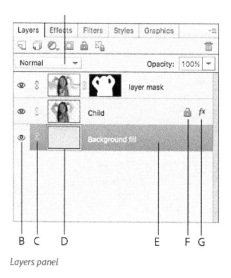

Layers panel

- Found on the right side, this panel allows users to manage layers, masks, and effects.

- Layer thumbnails make it easy to visualize changes.

5. Taskbar

- Positioned at the bottom, it offers quick actions like undo/redo, zoom, and navigation.

6. Organizer Integration

•   Accessible via a button in the taskbar, it connects to the Elements Organizer for browsing and managing files.

7. Contextual Menus

•   Right-clicking objects or layers brings up context-specific options for faster workflows.

8. Guided Edit Categories

•   Divided into sections like Basics, Fun Edits, Special Effects, and Photo Merge, making it easy to find relevant tutorials.

Organizing Your Workspace

It is therefore very important to organize your workspace so as to improve the effectiveness and the fun of photo editing. The interface of Photoshop Elements 2025 is adjustable to match a particular workflow of the user to a certain extent.

- By the Window option, user is able to hide/show specific panels such as layers, history and effects among others.

- Close many other panels in order to minimize their usage when not necessary. Drag the panels around the workspace to help yourself organize them better.

- Dock should reserve a part of its interface to frequently used panels which can be easily accessed.

- Click on Window on the top menu, then on Workspace as shown below and finally select Save Workspace as shown below.

- Name your workspace in order to access it later.

- On the menu, go to View and click on Toolbars and then choose customize.

- Burlap, sandpaper, axle grease, sheet metal screws, steel washers, water, WL-toothbrush, rags, old clothes and enjoyable photo editing. Photoshop Elements 2025 allows you to customize the interface to suit your workflow. Here's how:

1. Customize Panels and Tools

- Show/Hide Panels:

  - Use the Window menu to toggle visibility for panels like Layers, History, and Effects.

  - Close unnecessary panels to reduce clutter.

- Rearrange Panels:

  - Drag and drop panels to reposition them within the workspace.

  - Dock frequently used panels for easy access.

2. Save a Workspace Layout

- After arranging panels and tools to your preference, save the layout:

  - Go to Window > Workspace > Save Workspace.

  - Name your workspace for future use.

3. Adjust Toolbar

- Tools can be grouped or reorganized:

  - Right-click the toolbar and select Customize Toolbar.

  - Add, remove, or rearrange tools as needed.

4. Switch Between Modes

Photoshop Elements has three primary modes:

1. Quick: Basic format with core components included.

2.   Guided: Offers the diverse form of presentation of the certain process with indications on how it can be done.

3.   Expert: Show bars and icons of all the panels and gives access to all the additional sets of editing tools.

Toggle between modes from the "Mode" button on the top right corner of the workspace.

5. Adjust Screen Modes

- Switch display settings to focus on editing:

  - Standard Screen Mode: Hides all menus and task bars are hidden.

  - Full Screen with Menus: Efficient since the boxes occupy less space while the menus themselves are easily visible.

  - Full Screen Mode: Removes all border and backgrounds to give a clean view of what you're working on.

• Switch between the modes using the View > Screen Mode menu.

- Click on Window and pull down the list and select Workspace, a subheading appears and you click on Reset Workspace to get to the defaults editing.

Understanding File Types and Formats

Photoshop Elements 2025 is compatible with different file types and formats for helping when editing, exporting, and even sharing projects.

Original file mode when a Photoshop user opens a picture variety of file types and formats, allowing flexibility for editing, exporting, and sharing your work. Here's a detailed breakdown:

1. Common File Formats

- **PSD (Photoshop Document):**

  - Native file format for Photoshop. Retains layers, effects, and adjustments for further editing.

- Ideal for projects still in progress.

- **JPEG (Joint Photographic Experts Group):**

  - Compressed image format. Common for sharing online or printing.

  - Loses some quality due to compression.

- **PNG (Portable Network Graphics):**

  - Supports transparency and lossless compression.

  - Suitable for web graphics and logos.

- **TIFF (Tagged Image File Format):**

  - High-quality format with support for layers and transparency.

  - Often used in professional printing.

- **GIF (Graphics Interchange Format):**

  - Supports animations and simple graphics with limited colors.

- Suitable for short animations and web usage.

2. Specialized Formats

- **RAW:**

  - Unprocessed image data from cameras.

  - Requires processing using the Camera Raw plug-in for adjustments.

- **BMP (Bitmap):**

  - Uncompressed format with high detail.

  - Rarely used due to large file sizes.

- **HEIF/HEIC(High-Efficiency Image Format):**

  - High-quality format with smaller file sizes.

  - Supported on modern devices and useful for storage.

3. Export and Sharing Formats

- PDF (Portable Document Format):

- Useful for creating printable documents with embedded images.

- Supports vector and raster graphics.

- **MP4 (Video):**

  - If using photo slideshows or multimedia projects, MP4 is the preferred video export format.

- **WebP:**

  - Optimized for web use with high-quality compression.

4. Choosing the Right Format

- Editing and Flexibility: PSD or TIFF (all layers with layers and alpha channels).

- Web and Sharing: If with image, preferably JPEG or PNG format, compressed but very clear for common usage.

- Archiving: RAW or TIFF format (the format which retains all the image data).

- Animation: GIF (restricted motion graphics) or MP4 (enhanced picture galleries).

Creating New Projects

Photoshop Components 2025 gives a clear prepare for beginning modern ventures, whether you're altering a photo, making illustrations, or planning interactive media substance. Take after these steps:

Step 1:

Dispatch the Application

1. Open Photoshop Components and select Photo Editor from the Domestic Screen.

Step 2:

Begin a Unused Venture

1. Fast Begin:

- Within the Record menu, select Modern > Clear Record.

- On the other hand, tap Open to purport an existing photo for altering.

2. Guided Alter Begin:

- Explore to the Guided Mode tab and select from pre-designed formats or workflows.

3. Extend from Organizer:

- Get to your media in Components Organizer, select records, and tap Alter in Photoshop Components.

Step 3:

Design Project Settings

• **Within the Modern Report discourse box:**

- Preset Sizes: Select from choices like standard photo sizes, social media measurements, or custom sizes.

- Width & Tallness: Characterize the measurements in pixels, inches, or other units.

- Determination: Set the determination (e.g., 72 ppi for web, 300 ppi for print).

- Foundation Substance: Select a foundation color or straightforward.

  Step 4:

Spare Venture Settings

1. After setting up the extend, spare your work:
o   Go   to   Record   >   Spare   As.
o Select the required record organize

CHAPTER TWO

Importing and Organizing Photos

Importing Photos from Devices and Storage

Importing images is present in Photoshop Elements 2025 under multiple approaches for the purpose of simplifying the access to the images that you want to edit. Here's how you can import your photos:

1. Camera/Smartphone, or External Device Import

- If you have the Open Elements Organizer option on the iPod Home screen, select it.
- Go to the File menu and click on Import At the top of the screen select the device you want to import from (camera, smartphone, memory card, etc.).
- The Import Photos and Videos dialog box covers the screen with a preview of the images and videos that you wish to import.

- Select the import location (For instance, the desktop, the storage area, your hard drive or any other folder).o Click Import to import the files.
- You can also put pictures through the File options in the Photo Editor.
- Open Adobe Photoshop, go to select file and click Get Photos from camera then follow the wizard to import the photos. Devices and storage options, enabling easy access to your images for editing. Here's how you can import your photos:

1. Importing from a Camera, Smartphone, or External Device

- Using the Elements Organizer:

- Open Elements Organizer from the Home screen.
- Click Import at the top of the window and choose the device you want to import from (e.g., camera, smartphone, or memory card).

- The Import Photos and Videos dialog will appear, allowing you to select the files you want to import.
- Choose the import destination (e.g., your hard drive or an external storage location).
- Click Import to transfer the files.

- **Using the File Menu:**

- You can also import images directly from the File menu in the Photo Editor.
- Select File > Get Photos from Camera and follow the prompts to import your photos.

2. Importing from an External Drive (HDD, Flash drives etc)

- Thus to import images, one only needs to copy them from an external storage device such as a USB flash drive, an external hard disk, and and drop them to the element workspace.
- Go to File > Open and look for the location to your external drive or directory that contains the

photos enabling easy access to your images for editing.

3. Importing from Cloud Storage

• If you have cloud storage services like Adobe Cloud or Google Drive, you can sync your cloud storage with your computer and access those files:

- Open File > Open in Photoshop Elements.
- Navigate to your cloud storage folder on your computer and select the images to import.

4. From Social Networking sites and Online File Hosting Services

- Using the Organizer, you can link Photoshop Elements to your Facebook, flicker or other social networks.
- Elements to Facebook, Flickr, or other social media platforms through the Organizer. That way once the two are connected you can download images straight to the library.

- If you want to get pictures from social media or any cloud storage to your computer and in turn, transfer the images into photos, there are two available: The File/Open and File/ Get photos from camera tabs.

- Turn on a scanner and connect it to your computer Then go to File on the menu bar and select import ⇒ From Scanner.

- Click from the menu bar to start scanning the photos and importing them directly into the software:

- You can connect Photoshop Elements to Facebook, Flickr, or other social media platforms through the Organizer. Once connected, you can download images directly into your library.

• Manual Download:

o Download images from social media or cloud storage to your computer manually, then import them into Photoshop Elements using the File > Open or File > Get Photos from Camera options.

4. Importing from Scanners

• Using the Scan Option: o Connect a scanner to your computer and access it through Photoshop Elements via File > Import > From Scanner. o Follow the on-screen prompts to scan and import photos directly into the software.

Using the Organizer

The organizer in Photoshop Components 2025 may be effective device for overseeing, making, and getting to photos, recordings, and ventures. In arrange to encourage the streamlining of the current business and compensation, as well as to guarantee the smooth working of the expansive basic record library. Which strategy might be utilized for deciding the chief official officer?

1. Opening the Organizer

The Organizer can be bolted from the Domestic screen by selecting Organizer, or from the Record menu of the Photo Editor by selecting Record > Organize.
2. Bringing in Media

• To begin including your media:

o Tap Purport on the best menu: For bringing in photographs from your computer, outside difficult drive, or cloud, it chooses records and booklets. On the other hand, utilize a camera to require a picture specifically from a organized gadget such as a camera, a smartphone, or a memory card.

3. Organizing Media

• Making Collections: Tap on the Collections checkbox and select Make Collection. The display will back the bolster of a related photographic bunch joined.

• Tagging with Keywords: By selecting a drawing and selecting Record > Watchword Labeling ". This makes it conceivable to classify photos by subject indistinguishable to 'vacation ',' relatives ' ". ".

• Rating and Labeling:

o Rate your photographs on a scale from 1 to 5 stars. You will too include colored names to appear the position of the picture (e.g. , ruddy for 'edit ', green for advertised

4. Looking and Sorting Media

• Savvy Look: The organizer incorporates a capable look work. Utilize the look bar to discover photos by catchphrase, tag, record sort, or any other extra metadata (such as date or area).

• Sorting: List your basic discharges by explicit criteria, counting date, assessment, or other watchword, utilizing the sort choice within the Organizer board.

5. Altering and Upgrading Photographs: The organizer permits you to rapidly alter a picture by selecting a picture and the vital Quick Edit button. This permits fundamental changes such as brightness, scattering, and evacuation of redness. Press on a picture and select Alter within the Photo Editor to urge more progressed alters.

Sorting, Rating, and Tagging Photos

Photoshop Components 2025 extends the various methods of creating and viewing your photographic library, allowing you to quickly locate and manage your visuals. Screen, assessment, and tag are essential tools for streamlining your work flow and improving your photograph's usability.

1. Sorting Photos

– By Date: The photograph can remain on screen until the date it was taken, or else it is possible to locate photographs taken at specific intervals of epochs.

By name: you may view images alphabetically by file name, which is useful if you have a convention for naming files.

By rating or label: you can create a photograph based on their star rating or color label, allowing you to highlight your finest photographs or, alternatively, to classify them according to your needs.

By broadcasting: Type of image determined by the type of media, similar to a photograph, video, or PDF file.

To sort your photos:

- Go to the Organizer panel.

Using the Interpret menu or the 'Sort' button in the toolbar, select a kind by option.

2. Rating Photos

STAR RATINGS You may assign an evaluation to any photograph by selecting it and using the star rating system (1 to 5 stars) to indicate quality or value. It's a fast and effective way of ranking your pictures right now.

- Right-click on an image and choose Set Rating to assign stars.

- Alternatively, use the Rating options from the toolbar at the top.

3. Tagging Photos

• Keyword Tagging: Tagging photos with a keyword allows you to categorize them based on specific concepts (e.g. " vacation ", " tribe ", " landscape ". For a large photographic collection, this will be of particular use.

To tag a picture, select the picture and choose "File > Keyword Tagging" or use the "Organizer" keyword panel.

You can create new keywords and apply them to multiple photos at once.

• Location Tagging you can additionally add location facts to the photograph (identical to GPS coordinates or municipality names), which is helpful if you are creating travel photographs or other geographic content. Photographs can be tagged together with their location manually or via Geo-Tagging if their GPS data is implanted in the image.

4. Using Albums for Organization

Next screen, evaluate and label your photos; it's a good idea to group them into Albums in the Components Organizer. Albums allow you to create photographs based on common subjects, events, or even projects. You may create an album by selecting and dragging photos from your previous album, or by using the Album option.

5. Searching for Tagged Photo

Using the Search attribute to locate explicit pictures based on the words, evaluation, or another tag you have used. The present makes it possible to filter your library competently and quickly locate the person you are looking for.

Creating Albums and Folders

For proficient photo administration, it is vital to arrange your photo into a book and a booklet. Photoshop Viewpoints 2025 empowers you to form an collection and booklet to classify your media so simply can effectively find and alter your photo. Here's how to make and oversee a collection and booklet.

1. Making Collections: Collections encourage the creation of photos based on topics, endeavors, incidents, and give a heightened ocular and organized strategy for the organization of the library. Here's how to make an collection within the perspective organizer.

1. Open the Organizer: Dispatch Photoshop Factors and open the Figure Organizer from the Domestic screen or the Record menu.

2. Make an Unused Collection: Within the Organizer window, tap the Collections tab on the left-hand side.

- Tap the Make Modern Collection button (a organizer symbol with a also sign).

- Title your collection (e.g., "Excursion Photographs" or "Family Representations").

3. Include Photographs to the Collection: After making the collection, select the photographs you need to incorporate.

Drag and drop the ones from the later collection, or right-click the picture and select Include to collection.

4. Organize Photographs in Multiple Collections: A single photo may be found in a number of collections which don't have any copies. The present enables you to require the same photo over diverse subjects, e.g. 'Vacation' and 'Relatives').

2. Making Organizers for File Organization

The booklet gives a distinctive way to shape your news coverage, particularly for taking care of expansive collections by date or another sort of news. Here's how to create and utilize a booklet in Calculate Organizer.

1. Create a Organizer:

- Within the Organizer, click the Organizers tab on the cleared out.
- Right-click within the Organizers range and select Make Modern Organizer.
- Title the organizer (e.g., "2024 Photos" or "Wedding Album").

2. Include Records to Organizers:

- Drag and drop pictures from the Organizer into the recently made organizer.
- On the other hand, utilize the Purport alternative to moment photographs specifically into a particular organizer.

3. Organize Envelopes: By making subfolders, you'll make a booklet progressively. For instance, a fundamental book 'Vacation' can be went with by subfolders for a specific trip, which would something else be yearly.

3. Advantages of Collections vs. Organizers

• Collection:

- Excellent for creating regular collections of images based on themes or ventures.
- Photographs can appear in many collections without duplication.

Ideal for creating customized projects such as picture albums, slideshows, and collages.

• Envelopes: Ideal for sorting images according to record structure or capacity sections.

It is ideally suited to creating a large photographic collection by date, time, or camera type.

4. Managing Collections and Organizers

Renaming To change the label for the next organizer, right-click and choose Rename.

Right-click on the collection or booklet you want to remove, then choose Remove. The act of deleting a selection does not remove the original photograph; rather, it removes them from the collection.

Face Recognition and Tagging People

Photoshop components 2025 include powerful tools to identify faces and identify people in your photographs. This feature enables you to easily create and search your photographic library by recognizing and automatically labeling faces. Here is how to use this feature.

1. Face Recognition

Photoshop Components 2025 uses tackle recognition technology to involuntarily recognize and differentiate expressions in your photo. This makes it a lot easier to classify and locate images based on citizens in them.

•   Automatic Face Detection: When you import a photo into the Factor Organizer, Photoshop Factors scan the photo and detect expressions. Faces are marked with a small icon, indicating that the software has identified them.

•   Viewing Detected Faces: In the People view of the Organizer, you'll see all the detected faces grouped together. You can quickly browse through faces that have been identified in your photo collection.

2. Tagging People

Once the fingerprints are detected, you can place them next to the names of citizens in the photograph. The current is particularly helpful for the large photographic collection, as it allows you to search for explicit human beings.

- Manually Tagging Faces: In People view, click on a face in a photo. If you have already identified the person, you can either type their name or choose a name from the current tag if you have already identified them.

- Automatic Tagging Suggestions:

As you mark individuals in one photograph, Photoshop functions can propose labels for the same faces in different images. The present saves time by unconsciously recognizing the same being in a number of photographs.

- Adding Tags: If the encounter is detected but the word nay is not used unconsciously in academic writing, you may right-click on the encounter and choose Add Name to identify the human.

o You may also create a citizen tag in the collection (e.g. " House ", " Friend ", etc.) For a more simplified organization.

3. Searching by People

As soon as you have a tag condition on your photograph, Photoshop components allow you to easily locate the image of the person you are looking for.

•   Search by Name: Enter a name for an entity in the search bar of the Organizer. All photographs of the human will be exposed by the software wherever he seems to be.

•   Smart Search: You can refine your search by using terms, tags, or even evaluation, which makes it easier to locate photographs of precise citizens in your library.

4. Managing Face Tags

•   Reviewing Face Tags: Photoshop features also allow you to edit and critique encounter tags. You can manually correct the tag, or you can remove it if the software mistakenly identified a human.

• Merging Duplicate Tags: Assumes that a different tag has been created for the same entity (e.g. , one for 'John Doe'and another for 'John D. '. "), you can group them to keep your library shape.

Backup and Restore Options

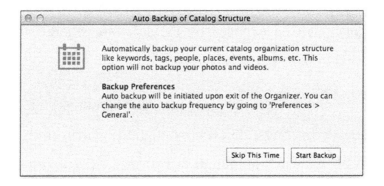

Photoshop Components 2025 gives a capable way to guarantee your work, counting media records, ventures, and altering story, is safely reinforcement. These reinforcement capacities are crucial to ensure your photo, alters, and other data in case of auxiliary intrusion or coincidental misfortune. Here's how to utilize the reinforcement and reestablish work.

1. Reinforcement Your Catalog

Each of your metadata, such as labels, assessment, alters, collections, and ventures, is put away within the Photoshop Catalogue. You'll keep it overhauled routinely to anticipate information misfortune in your catalog.

• How to Back Up Your Catalog:

1. Open Components Organizer.

2. Go to Alter > Inclinations (Windows) or Photoshop Components > Inclinations (Mac).

3. Within the Common tab, beneath Catalog alternatives, select Reinforcement.

4. Select your favored reinforcement recurrence (day by day, week after week, month to month, or physically).

5. Select an area on your computer or an outside drive to store the reinforcement.

6. Press Alright to affirm your reinforcement settings. MANUAL Reinforcement MANUAL Reinforcement

can be gotten by going by the FILE>BACKUP CATEGORIES AND SELECTING A Reinforcement Area.

2. Backing up Media Records

In spite of the fact that the catalog measurements are basic, you'd moreover like to bolster the genuine media record (photographs and videos). Photoshop perspectives don't suddenly back up communication records, so it is basic to utilize outside difficult drives or cloud reinforcement arrangements for this reason.

• Reinforcement Media Records Utilizing Outside Capacity:

1. Select the media files you need to back up in the Components Organizer.

2. Physically duplicate and glue them onto outside difficult drives, USB drives, or something else into the cloud.

• Cloud Reinforcement In the event that you have got an Adobe description, you'll be able synchronize your news record to the Adobe Cloud and bolster your photo virtual. The display gives a secure and available strategy of ensuring your picture and altering your content.

3. Reestablishing Your Catalog

In the event that you need to reestablish your catalog payable due to organizational issues or information misfortune, Photoshop components give a basic rebuilding alternative.

• How to Reestablish a Reinforcement Catalog:
1. Open Components Organizer.

2. Go to Record > Reestablish Catalog.

3. Explore to the area where your backup catalog is put away.

4. Select the reinforcement record and press Open.

5. The catalog will be reestablished, and your metadata (labels, collections, evaluations, etc.) will be recouped.

4. Restoring Media Files

To restore a communication file, you need to recover the file from a backup location (external storage or cloud assistance) and reintegrate it into the aspects of the Organizer.

- **Steps to Restore Media Files:**

1. If your files are stored externally or in a cloud service, you can copy them back to your computer.

2. To re-import photos to the Factor Organizer, use File > Get Photo Folders and Files.

3. If you're using Adobe Cloud, sync the files from the cloud to your local machine.

5. Best Practices for Backup

Regular backup agenda Determine your catalog backup agenda to ensure that you wear 'thymine lose valuable metadata, such as edits else tags.

Using multiple Backup Locations to store your Backup Catalogue equally on a personal and external drive, or using a cloud service for added security.

Occasionally, it is a good idea to test restore a backup every so often to make sure that the procedure runs smoothly if you need it.

CHAPTER THREE

Basic Photo Editing

Understanding Quick, Guided, and Expert Modes in Photoshop Elements 2025

Photoshop factors 2025 has three essential alter modes: The Quick, Controlled, and Master Plan, depending on the buyer's competence and the corresponding adjustment, provides unique levels of restriction and ease of use.

1. Fast Mode: is best suited for novice customers who need to make quick changes with little effort.

- It gives essential apparatuses for editing, altering presentation, and improving color.
- It offers an instinctive interface with programmed alterations and easy-to-apply channels.

2. Guided Mode:

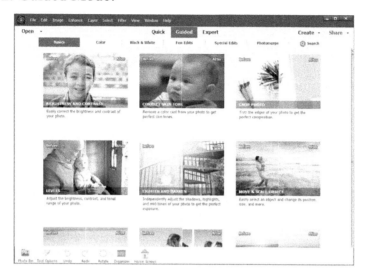

Perfect for customers who require further regulation above their changes but still require instructions.

The Photoshop circuit board provides a basic, easy-to-follow interface for removing blemishes, adding text, or any other object in order to produce a photographic output. It could be a remarkable center of gravity, promoting joint simplicity and improved efficiency.

3. Master Mode: It gives packed reach to all the advanced devices and spotlights in Photoshop Components.

Its superior suit for other experienced customers who need to completely regulate above their neutering. Permits for gritty alterations utilizing layers, covers, and channels.

Cropping, Straightening, and Resizing in Photoshop Elements 2025

These are essential editing tools for improving the composition and presentation of your photos:

1.   Cropping: Allows you to trim unnecessary parts of the image, focusing on the subject. Using the Crop tool to select a location you wish to maintain. If necessary, you can adjust the aspect ratio, use a predefined ratio, or perform a freehand cut.

2.   Straightening: Helps correct tilted or crooked images by adjusting the angle. It uses the Straightening Device to draw a line parallel to the rim of the photograph, which should remain horizontal or vertical, and the innovation naturally revolves the image in order to straighten it.

3.   Resizing: Essential for adjusting the dimensions of your photo. Use the Resize device to select the exact size, then adjust the printer resolution, then use the

Web browser. You may extend the image, otherwise depressed, depending on your request, as the preservation of the dimension ratio will never occur otherwise.

Adjusting Exposure, Brightness, and Contrast in Photoshop Elements 2025

This adjustment will help you manage the light and tonic range of your photograph, allowing you to create an extra visual appeal.

1. Exposure: Controls the overall lightness or darkness of the image. It employs the Exposure Skidder to increase or decrease the exposure, helping to repair underexposed or overexposed photographs.

2. Brightness: It changes the intensity of the entire pixel in the image, making it either brighter or darker, which does not change the shadow or emphasize it. The Brightness Scander may be used to adjust the brightness of the image as a whole.

3. Contrast: It alters the distinction of light and dark areas in the image, making it appear to

be more or less flat. It employs a difference skidder to magnify details by increasing the gap between shadows and simultaneously minimizing the difference to produce a soft form.

White Balance and Color Corrections

For your photographs to have precise colors, you need white harmony and color correction. At the same time, it supports correct color imbalance caused by different lighting conditions, such as tungsten, fluorescent, or daylight.

1. White Balance

The white level ensures that the colors in your photograph appear natural and real; so that they appear to be alive, remove all of the color casts caused by the light source. Different light sources may give your pictures a shade, and adjusting the white stability may be helpful in removing it.

• Self-regulating White Evenness The Auto White proportion feature of Photoshop tries to correct the spontaneously established color cast above the image's light. This may be useful in a quick adaptation when the photograph was taken under supervision of changes or unusual light.

Manual award of White Symmetries in the Expert Mode, you may manually adjust the white evenness using the White Proportion tool.

Click on the White Poise icon (the eyedropper icon) and select a portion of the image that should remain white, otherwise impersonal gray. To moderate the color, the Photoshop components will adjust the entire image.

You can also use Skidder Enjoy Temperature (blue to yellow) and Tint (green to magenta) to manually adjust the white balance.

Using presets in Photoshop components allows you to set up presets for common lighting conditions such as daylight, cloudy, tungsten, fluorescent, and custom options. For simple use, these presets can remain in the Quick Mode or Steering Mode.

2. Color Corrections

Color correction is the process of adjusting the colors in your image so that they appear more natural or in order to achieve a precise hue or effect. Photoshop Factors 2025 extends various color correction techniques.

• Adjusting Saturation: Saturation controls color intensity. You may continue to use the Saturation Skidder to increase or decrease the transparency of your colors, thereby reducing the excess graphic or tonality.

In Quick Mode or Expert Mode, apply the Vibrance and Saturation sliders to adjust the color intensity of the image generally.

• Using the HSL Panel (Hue, Saturation, Luminance):

In the Expert Mode, the HSL panel (Hue, Saturation, Luminance) allows you to adjust the details of the image. You can adjust the color of the object (such as blues and turquoises and reds and oranges and so on), manage their intensities (intensity), and adjust their brightness (lightness).

• Using the Color Curves: The Curves device in the Expert Mode allows for progressive color correction. It allows you to adjust the tonic range and color proportion in the entire image, as well as the explicit color channels (red,green,blue). The current will allow you to fine-tune your image's contrast and color balance for a more precise expression.

• Auto Color Correction: In Quick Mode, you can apply Auto Color Correction, which analyses the image and corrects the color to improve the overall tone and color balance. For users who want a quick and simple color improvement, this is a one-click solution.

Red Eye Removal and Spot Healing in Photoshop Elements 2025

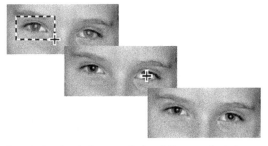

Correct red eye by selecting an eye (top) or clicking an eye (center).

1 To manually fix red eye, select the Eye tool 👁 in **Quick** or **Advanced** mode.

2 In the **Tool Options** bar, set the **Pupil Radius** and **Darken Amount**.

3 In the image, do one of the following:

- Select a red area of an eye.
- Draw a selection over the eye area.

When you release the mouse button, the red is removed from the eyes.

The common photo modifying devices in Photoshop are ruddy eye evacuation and the recuperating of the topographic focuses, which offer assistance to improve the image's depiction and dispose of any imperfections.

1. Ruddy Eye Expulsion: Redeyes are common in streak photography, whereabouts the moment understudy looks ruddy in arrange that the streak echoes off the retina. An essential device for expelling ruddy eye from photos is displayed in Photoshop angles.

• How to Utilize the Ruddy Eye Evacuation Instrument:

1. Open your picture in Components Editor.
2. From the toolbar, select the Ruddy Eye Remover. The instrument makes the eye show up with a ruddy line another to it.

3. Press on the ruddy eyes of the photo. Photoshop's components will naturally seek for ruddy eyes and supplant them with an extra natural dim understudy.
4. If necessary, you will alter Understudy Measure or Obscurity within the tool's choice barroom for more exact impacts. The device works enough, particularly when the red-eye is concentrated and straightforward to distinguish, but manual alteration may still be fundamental within the case of complex photos.

2. Spot Recuperating Brush Instrument: To expel flaw, tidy bugs, or any undesirable highlights from your photo, the Spot Mending Brush is planned. To flawlessly mix flaw within the environment, it employments a sample pixel from the complete area.

• How to Utilize the Spot Recuperating Brush Instrument:

1. Select the Spot Mending Brush Device from the toolbar (the band-aid symbol).

2. Utilize the bracket key ([to diminish,] to extend) or the barroom option to alter the brush estimate.

3. Tap the flaw you would like to evacuate, or then again, destroy it. The Photoshop angles will spontaneously fill within the zone with pixels from the following picture. You'll alter the way the instrument works based on the sort of defect you evacuate.

5. In case fundamental, utilize the Clone Stamp or the Recuperating Brush to treat other complex musca volitans with more prominent skin defect.

Applying Filters and Effects in Photoshop Elements 2025

You can quickly change the image's expression and feeling with the filter and the result. A number of innovative filters and effects are available in Photoshop to enhance or stylize your images.

1. Using Filters

There is a great variety of filters that can be applied to your photos in Photoshop. The filter may adjust the overall tone, texture, or may produce an estethic effect.

- How to Apply Filters:

1. Navigate to the Filter section of the main menu and browse by type, e.g. Artistic, Blur, Noise, Sharpen, etc. :).

2.   Select a filter you want to apply.

3.   Adjust the settings in the options bar (some filters have sliders for intensity, radius, etc.).

4.   Click OK to apply the filter.

Some of the most popular filters include:

•   Gaussian Blur for softening the image.

•   Oil Paint for a painted look.

•   Sharpen to bring out details in the photo.

•   Noise filters for adding a textured or grainy effect.

2. Applying Effects

Effects are commonly defined places that alter the color, tone, and texture of a photographic image to produce a conventional appearance. A number of predefined effects which can be applied to an image together with an individual flaw are available in the Photoshop effects.

- How to Apply Effects:

1. Open the Effects panel (found in Expert Mode or Quick Mode).

2. Browse the available effects, which are categorized (e.g., Black and White, Vintage, Vignette, etc.).

3. Click on the effect you would like to implement in practice. Alternatively, depending on the preset, you can adjust its robustness.

Assuming you desire a unified effect of a number of impacts, merely exploit the individual effects and then add more people to the top.

The consequences are particularly helpful in improving the portrayal, adding resourcefulness, or in creating an imaginative atmosphere in the photograph.

CHAPTER FOUR

Advanced Editing and Retouching

Working with Layers and Layer Styles

Apply a layer style

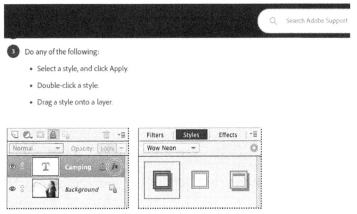

A style icon indicates a layer style is applied to the layer.

If you don't like the result, press Ctrl+Z (Command + Z in Mac OS) to remove the style, or choose Edit > Undo.

Layers are the mainstay of primarily image editing in Photoshop's factors which allow non-destructive editing and provide flexibility in the way in which compositional elements interact with one another. Layer Styles are predefined effects which can be applied to layers in order to produce a variety of eye outcomes. Here is a brief outline of how to work together with both of them.

1. Working with Layers

Layers in Photoshop's features allow you to separate components of an image, such as text, shape, and adjustment. This makes it easier to edit human parts in an image that does not move between people.

- Creating New Layers:

To generate a recent layer, travel to Layer > recent > Recent, or alternatively use a recent layer icon on the Layers panel. You may choose from several layers, such as space, text, or an alternatively a contour layer.

- Selecting Layers:

To select a layer, click on it in the Layers panel. Additionally, you may choose a number of layers by holding the transition and pressing the layer you wish to include.

- Moving Layers:

- You can move over a layer by selecting it and then using the Move device (v) to drag it to a previous situation. The layer system, together with the layer over the prime existing visible above that below, alters the appearance of the image.

• **Visibility and Locking Layers:** Layer can be hidden by snapping the eye icon near the layer in the Layers panel. It's useful if you want to emphasize certain parts of your composition. Snap the lock icon at the top of the Layers panel to prevent accidental changes.

• **Layer Masks:**

The Layer Mask allows you to hide a portion of a layer which is not permanently deleted. To create a mask, click on the Add Layer Mask button at the bottom of the Layers panel and then use the brush to draw black or white on the location of the mask.

2. Layer Styles

Layer Styles are predefined effects which can be used to layer in order to provide the unique properties of descent shadow, freshness, bevel, and other ocular effects. These results are able to be adjusted and non-destructive, which means that they can be changed afterwards without changing the original layer.

- How to Apply Layer Styles:

1. Select the layer you want to apply a style to in the Layers panel.

2. Go to Layer > Layer Style and choose a ramification similar to Shadow, Bevel, and Emboss, or Outer Glow.

3. In the pop-up book window that looks like this. For instance, you may adjust the angle of the shadow that descends, or adjust the transparency of the outer freshness.

- Common Layer Styles:

Drop Shadow: It adds a shadow to the object in the layer so that it hides from the surroundings.

Outer Glow: Applies a soft, glowing edge to the layer.

Inner Glow: Adds a glow effect inside the layer's boundaries.

Bevel & Emboss: Creates a raised or recessed effect, giving the illusion of depth.

Stroke adds a boundary line approximately the layer which can be personalized with different colours and thicknesses.

Editing Layer Styles:

To get the background and create transformations close to all intervals, double-click on the Layer Style influence in the Layers panel. This makes it possible to make simple adaptations without the need to modify the resulting situation.

Copying Layer Styles:

If you want to apply the same effect to the next layer, you can copy and paste layers in the following way. Right-click the layer in question, choose Copy Layer Style, then right-click another layer and choose Paste Layer Style.

Blending Modes

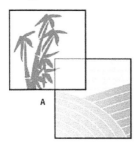

Blending layers

Mixing Modes and Cloning/Healing instruments are exceptionally vital in Photoshop angles 2025; they permit you to imaginatively control layers and settle flaw in your pictures. A brief depiction of how these gadgets work and how they can be utilized competently is given underneath.

Mixing modes are utilized to decide the way in which two layers (or components) blend together. They decide how the pixels of the oinnacle layer associated with the pixels of the verifiable in layer, permitting you to create a wide extend of impacts from a tricky alteration that can lead to emotional changes.

How to Utilize Mixing Modes:

1. Select the layer you need to apply the mixing mode to.

2. The default esteem for the drop-down menu another to the oinnacle within the Layers board is Ordinary. ".

3. Tap on this drop-down to uncover a list of accessible Mixing Modes.

Sorts of Mixing Modes:

- Typical: The default layer is laid down in a way that does not blend, where the beat layer totally covers the foot layer.

- Duplicate the pixel colors of the primary layer with the ones underneath them to form the picture darker. This may be valuable in making shadows or obscuring a picture in an substitute way. Screen lights the picture by rearranging and increasing pixel colors, making it idealize for highlighting on the other hand shinning pictures.

Overlay: Combines Increase and Screen, upgrading differentiate by obscuring shadows and brightening highlights. Delicate light, which is valuable for delicate alteration of distinction, darkens or helps the image, which is established within the colors of the primary layer.

Difficult Light: Comparative to Overlay, but with more concentrated, including a more discernible differentiate impact. Differentiate by expelling the colors from the layer, you make a tall differentiate impact. The current can deliver solitary, unique discoveries.

Down to earth Employments:

Imaginative Impacts: Utilize Overlay or Delicate Light to improve surface and profundity in imaginative compositions.

Mixing Surfaces: Apply Increase to mix surfaces or shadows into your picture for more authenticity.

Cloning and Healing Tools

The Cloning and Mending devices were created to expel undesirable parts of a picture, such as flaws, clean, or other visual diversions, whereas flawlessly mixing in with the rest of the picture.

Cloning Devices

The Clone Stamp device permits you to test pixels from one portion of your picture and paint them onto another portion, effectively cloning surfaces, colors, and points of interest.

How to Utilize:

1. Select the Clone Stamp Device from the toolbar.
2. Keep the Alt key (Alternative over Mac) and hit the spot you would like to test.

3. Let go of the Alt crucial and paint over the zone you want to supplant utilizing the tested pixel.

4. Alter the brush estimate and hardness for a more exact clone.

• Common sense Employments:

- Evacuating flaws or objects within the foundation.
- Copying components (such as designs or surfaces) in your picture.

Mending Devices

Spot Mending Brush The Spot Recuperating Brush naturally mixes the examined area with the encompassing pixels, so it's idealize for fast expulsion of minor blemish without concern almost cloning correct pixel insights.

How to Utilize:

1. Select the Spot Recuperating Brush Apparatus from the toolbar.

2. Essentially press or drag over the range you would like to repair. In arrange to conceal the blemish, Photoshop components haphazardly test from adjacent pixels and mix them together. Depending on the complexity of the area to be repaired, you'll be able switch between Content-Aware (using adjoining pixels) and Nearness parallel (test adjacent zones) for

superior comes about. The Recuperating Pencil The Healing Pencil is comparative to the Spot Recuperating Pencil, but it permits you to physically select the root locale to be inspected, giving you more control after the blending and patch strategy. **How to Utilize:**

1. Select the Recuperating Brush Device. 2. Hold Alt (Alternative on Mac) to test a clean range. 3. Paint over the zone you need to recuperate, mixing the adjustment consistently.

• Down to earth Employments: Settling skin flaws or little flaws in representations. Repairing harmed photo zones or evacuating diversions like clean spots.

Skin Smoothing and Enhancements

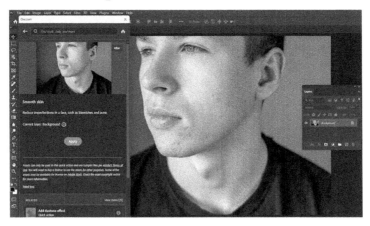

Skin smoothing and improvement are basic to improve the appearance of the skin whereas keeping up its normal surface. Photoshop perspectives 2025 gives numerous apparatuses and frameworks to realize the abovementioned comes about, centering on subtlety and reasonable introduction of the center.

1. Skin Smoothing Strategies: The smooth skin includes decreasing the appearance of discoloration, wrinkles, and other surrenders whereas keeping up key subtle elements such as skin surface and natural facial highlights.

Utilizing the Spot Recuperating Brush The Spot

Mending Brush could be a perfect tool to expel little abandons such as skin break out, spots, and imperfections. It'll actually mix in with the encompassing skin tone.

How to Utilize:

1. Select the Spot Recuperating Brush Device (band-aid symbol).

2. Alter the brush measure to coordinate the estimate of the blemish.

3. Tap on the something else undesirable musca volitans to actually expel them, permitting Photoshop to test the encompassing range. Utilizing the Healing brush device for more exact redresses, the Healing brush instrument permits you to choose a beginning locale from which to draw a test, gift improved handles past the surfaces and the skin tone. **How to Utilize:**

1. Select the Recuperating Brush Apparatus from the toolbar.

2. Hold Alt (Choice on Mac) to test a clean range of the skin.

3. Paint over the flaws to smooth them out, mixing them consistently with the encompassing skin. Utilizing Gaussian Obscure to smooth the surface of another uniform skin tone, Gaussian Obscure can exist commonplace with, in spite of the fact that it is vital to utilize selectively to avoid oversmoothing.

How to Utilize:

1. Copy the image layer.

2. Apply Gaussian Obscure (Channel > Obscure > Gaussian Obscure) to the copied layer.
3. Include a layer cover so that the film is over the layer, and utilize a delicate brush to dismantle the exterior regions Don' thymine requests smooth, such as the eyes and lips.

Tip:

Apply a inconspicuous obscure (moo span) to dodge excessively delicate skin.

2. Upgrades for Skin Tone and Surface: Once the skin is smooth, upgrades can advance upgrade the appearance, include plangency, redress unequal tone, and allow the skin an inalienable freshness. Altering the skin tone with Hue/Saturation The Hue/Saturation adjustment layer empowers you to attain a uniform skin color. This apparatus may be accommodating in case the skin has an unnatural color.

Selective Color Adjustments

Selective Color Adjustment in Photoshop aspects allows you to give priority to and enhance specific colors in an image while leaving other people unaffected. This is particularly helpful when you want to create a confident component position beyond otherwise correct color imbalances without changing the entire image. There are several methods to perform selective color correction in Photoshop components 2025 below.

1. Using the Hue/Saturation Adjustment Layer

The Hue/Saturation adjustment layer allows you to control the brightness of human colors in the image, thus becoming one of the most common methods of selective color correction.

• How to Use:

1. Select Layer > New Adjustment Layer > Hue/Saturation.

2. In the Qualities panel, click on the drop-down menu labeled Edit and select the color you want to modify (e.g. Red, Blue, and Green).

3. To adjust the selected color, use the Hue, Saturation, and Lightness sliders. Hue changes color, Saturation adjusts its intensity, and Lightness brightens or darkens. You may also use the Targeted Adjustment Tool (the grasp icon) to snap directly to the image and adjust the color in real time.

• Practical Example:

If you want to make the sky bluer, choose blues from the Edit menu and increase the Saturation to increase the blue hue.

2. Using the Selective Color Adjustment Tool (Selective Color)

The Selective Color Adjustment allows you to fine-tune individual color components such ascyan, magenta, yellow, etc.) in a clear color range.

- How to Use:

1. Go to Layer > New Adjustment Layer > Selective Color.

2. Select a color variety you would like to modify in the Quality Panel, for instance. , Red, Yellow, and Neutral).

3. To change the intensity of a particular color within the selected area, adjust the slider for Cyan, Magenta, Yellow, and Black.

- Practical Example:

To warm up the skin tone, choose reds and adjust the yellow skidder to increase the heat, or adjust the magenta skidder for a more balanced expression.

3. Using the Color Replacement Tool

Another way to selectively adjust color in the exact regions of the image is using the Color Matching Tool. It works by painting over the existing colors, together with fresh ones, which may be useful for more precise handling than color changes.

*   How to Use:

1. Select the Color Replacement Tool from the toolbar (shortcut: Shift+B).

2. Select the color you wish to change and select the sampling option (continuous, once or otherwise context Swatch).

3. In order to change the color, the paint will go over the areas you wish, and the tool will replace the chosen color with the new one.

• Practical Example: You may use this tool to replace a red shirt with a green one by sampling the red and painting over the area so as to replace it with the green one.

4. Using the Gradient Map Adjustment Layer for Color Control

The Gradient Map Adjustment Layer enables you to apply a gradient color scheme to your image, which is anchored in its own tonic range, resulting in an original and dramatic effect.

• How to Use:

1. Select Layer > New Adjustment Layer > Gradient Map.

2. Click on the gradient bar to edit the gradient, choose or create a gradient that fits your desired color change.

3. Adjust the gradient's position and blend mode to control how the gradient affects the image.

•   Practical Example: For shadows, you can use a cool gradient (blue-green) and a warm gradient (orange-yellow) to create conventional color significance.

5. Using the Channel Mixer for Advanced Color Adjustments

The Channel Mixer adjustment has a further progressive restriction that allows you to create custom color effects or correct color imbalances.

•   How to Use:

1.   Go to Layer > New Adjustment Layer > Channel Mixer.

2. To change the amount of the respective color channels in the image, adjust the slider for the red, green, and blue channels.

3.   Use the Monochrome checkbox to create black-and-white images with custom color channel weighting.

• Practical Example: It uses the Channel Mixer to alter the overall color symmetries of an image, such as changing a green image to a more impersonal tone by reducing its control over the Green Channel.

Using the Smart Brush

The Photoshop Factors 2025 Smart Brush allows you to quickly and precisely adjust an image anchored in a predefined way, such as color enhancement, distinction, or sharpness in the details. Involuntarily, the Smart brush detects the type of paint you exceed and uses the appropriate adjustment.

• How to Use:

1. Select the Smart Brush Tool from the toolbar (shortcut: K).

2. Choose the effect you would like to use (e.g. , Skin Smoothing, Vivid Color, Details.

3. Adjust the Size and Feather of the brush as needed.

4. Paint over the area you wish to adjust, and the Smart Brush will apply the selected result to that location, keeping the location of the adjustment.

• Practical Example: To improve sky colors in a panorama, choose Vivid Color and paint beyond the sky. The device will apply impregnating and planning to the sky without touching any part of the image.

Using the Selection Tools

The selection tools in Photoshop components play an important role in isolating a particular locality in the image, allowing the use of adjustments, outcomes, or other edits which do not significantly affect the rest of the picture. Here are the main choices available.

• Lasso Tool: The Lasso tool allows you to create a freeform selection around the image. It is perfect for choosing an irregular shape, or for a locality where a precise outline is never necessary.

How to Use:

1. Select the Lasso Tool from the toolbar (shortcut: L).

2. Click and drag to draw around the area you want to select.

3. Close the selection by connecting the endpoint to the starting point.

Practical Example: Use the Lasso Tool to select a portion of a subject's face for color adjustment.

The Polygonal Lasso Utensil This version of the Lasso utensil allows you to select straight lines by snapping in the direction you wish to select.

How to Use:

Select the Polygonal Lasso Tool from the toolbar.

1. Click near the place where you wish to select the straight line. To close the selection, double-click it.

Practical Example: Use it to select architectural elements or geometric shapes in an image.

The Magnetic Lasso device senses the edge of the image and automatically selects the one closest to it, thereby facilitating the selection of zones with a distinct edge, similar to the object against a solid background.

How to Use:

Select the Magnetic Lasso Tool from the toolbar.

1. Click on the selection to select it, then drag it along the edge of the selected object. As soon as you move, the device involuntarily snaps to the edge of the object.

Practical Example: Use the Magnetic Lasso tool to quickly select the outline of an entity or object, at the same time as a clear boundary.

The Quick Selection Tool The Quick Selection Tool allows you to select paint over a specified area. The apparatus spontaneously extends the selection to include the same pixel, which makes it perfect for selecting areas with uniform textures or alternative colors.

How to Use:

Select the Quick Selection Tool from the toolbar (shortcut: W).

1. Paint outside the area you wish to select, and the apparatus will instinctively locate the edge and expand the options.

Practical Example: Use it to select and improve the second shirt of the creature while leaving the rest of the picture unaltered.

Removing and Replacing Backgrounds

Setting expulsion and substitution are one of the foremost common operations for picture altering. Photoshop Variables 2025 make it basic to confine a subject and alter the foundation in an then again quenched way. Expel foundation with Fast Determination or Enchantment Wand for foundation evacuation. You will select the environment utilizing the instruments over, at that point expel or supplant it with another picture.

How to Expel:

1. Utilize the Quick Choice Instrument or Enchantment Wand Instrument to choose the foundation.

2. Refine the determination utilizing the Refine Edge or Select and Veil highlight for cleaner edges.

3. Hit Erase or include a Layer Veil to stow away the foundation.

Supplant foundation: Following, evacuate settings, at that point utilize layer to embed a later one. Essentially adhere a modern setting layer over the subject matter and alter the composition and lighting, in the event that necessary.

How to Supplant:

1. Expel the initial foundation utilizing the strategies over.

2. Embed a modern foundation by dragging the required picture onto the canvas.

3. Resize, position, and mix the new background with the subject for a consistent see.

• Down to earth Illustration: Employments the Enchantment Wand gadget to choose white, expel it, and supplant it with a colorful slope alternatively scenic picture for a qualified coating.

CHAPTER FIVE

Working with Text and Typography

Adding and Formatting Text in Photoshop Elements 2025

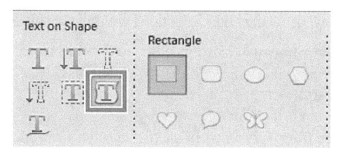

Text on Shape tool

Photoshop Components 2025, which includes and creates a basic appearance, together with a device component and a custom appearance option. Here's a step-by-step outline of how to include and preface it.

1. Including Content

• How to Include Content:

1. Select the Sort Device from the toolbar (easy route: T).

2. Tap anyplace on your canvas where you need the content to start.

3. Begin writing your content.

When the text is entered, you will remain competent to display it using the selection within the pleasant Gadget alternative barroom at the top of the screen.

Text style:

Select from a assortment of textual styles introduced on your framework.

Measure - change the measure taken by entering an esteem, or use an up and down lightning bolt.

Fashion: Select striking, italic, or normal fashion, depending on the textual style.

To get to the color picker and select the text color you want, imperativeness in the color test.

Applying Text Effects in Photoshop Elements 2025

A number of text effects that allow you to create text that stands outside, together with shadow, stroke, and other stylish enhancements, are available in the Photoshop components.

1. Drop Shadow

Using the Text layer, navigate to the Layer > Layer Style > Drop Shadow.

•   Adjust the shadow's opacity, distance, and size to create depth.

2. Outer Glow and Bevel

Moreover, from the Layer Style menu, you may also apply effects such as Outer Glow or Bevel & Emboss. The above-mentioned consequences allow you to create a radiance, otherwise undisguised, implication in your text.

•   Adjust settings for glow color, spread, size, and angle to suit the look you desire.

3. Stroke Effect

• Add a stroke to your text to create a border around it. You can set the stroke color, thickness, and situation (outside, inside, or another focus).

Creating Custom Text Styles

To create a custom text manner that can be used in different text components, you can recover the effects that you have applied to text as a manner.

1. Saving a Text Style:

• After applying the desired effects, go to Window > Styles to open the Styles panel.

To restore the current text style, click the Novel Style button at the bottom of the panel.

Currently, you may use this method to create an alternative text layer by selecting it from the Styles panel.

CHAPTER SIX

Special Effects and Filters

Channels and Results in Photoshop Components 2025 are capable instruments that permit you to control and upgrade your pictures in inventive ways. They can be utilized for everything from tricky improvement to emotional advancement, permitting you to explore with a wide run of strategies and impacts in arrange to grant your photo an unmistakable appearance. Channels in Photoshop Components 2025, the channel could be a pre-designed impacts those employments changes to your picture in expansion to express parts. The channel may change the common appearance of the picture, include aesthetics, or something else mimics photographic strategies.

• **Common Channels:**

Obscure is utilized to mellow the layout and make a feeling of movement. Gaussian Obscure, Movement Obscure, and Focal point Obscure are common choices.

Hone: Upgrades points of interest in an picture,

making it crisper and more characterized. Misshape Twists something else spreads the picture; permit you to appreciate the Spherize something else Spin channel in arrange to create a result. Commotion coordinating grain or arbitrariness into an picture, usual to results like Include Clamor or diminish Commotion. Imaginative mimics portray, drawing, or other elective craftsmanship setups along side the channel appreciate Oil Paint, Watercolor, and Blurb Edges.

• How to Apply Channels:

1. Select the layer you need to apply the channel to.
2. Navigate to Channel within the best menu and choose the required channel from the list.
3. Alter settings utilizing the slider and see the result. Tap Alright to apply the channel. The channel can moreover be utilized non-destructively by changing the picture layer to a Keen Protest, which permits you to adjust or expel the filter's noteworthiness afterward.

Using the Effects Panel

The Results Board of Photoshop angles 2025 gives a straightforward way to apply pre-made impacts to your pictures, subsequently encouraging the creation of stylish effects without the have to be physically alter the environment.

• How to Utilize the Impacts Board:

1. Open the Effects panel by selecting Window > Impacts from the beat menu.

2. You'll be able select from a assortment of impacts sorts, such as Photo impacts, Aesthetic comes about, and Surfaces, within the board.

3. To utilize the suggestion, fair pull up the moment thumbnail of the impact. The noteworthiness of the current picture will proceed to be utilized as an substitute layer, and you will be able to see the impact in genuine time.

4. In expansion to customizing the result utilizing the choice within the Results Board, you will utilize the Alter Skidder to improve the impact.

• Sorts of Impacts Accessible:

Photographic impacts which incorporate definitive visuals such as Dark and White, Dynamic, Sepia, and different ancient impacts.

Creative Impacts: These impacts mirror aesthetic styles such as Oil Portray, Watercolor, and Pencil Portray.

Surface combines surfaces such as canvas, grain, and metallic to create a assortment of surfaces on the image.

Custom impacts: The alter skidder permits you to alter the concentrated and characteristics of the utilized repercussion, as well as to supply adaptability and control. For occasion, you will alter the sum, Brightness, or Immersion of the photo a while later in arrange to be similar to the common way in which you center.

Blur, Sharpen, and Distort Filters in Photoshop Elements 2025

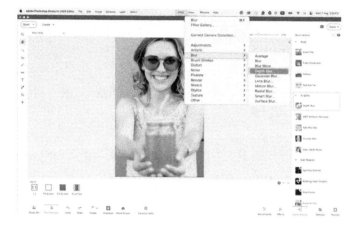

Photoshop Components 2025 gives a wide run of obscure, hone, and twisting channels that can altogether change the appearance of your photos, whether you need to form a delicate center, increment sharpness, or include stylish twisting.

1. Obscure Channels

The obscure channel mollifies the points of interest of the picture, permitting you to decrease the clamor, make a marvelous impact, or mimic motions.
• Gaussian Obscure: A smooth, indeed film over that's regularly utilized to mollify the picture or to decrease

the sharpness of the zone concerned. Movement Obscure copies the movement of a film over an picture in a company with a particular point utilized to get it the speed or enlightening.

• Focal point: Obscure to imitate the shallow profundity of the plot's results seen through the focal point, culminate for mirroring reasonable center comes about and bokeh. Spiral Obscure makes a hazy impact that mirrors the development of the camera or zooming, valuable for making a turning or zooming impact on pictures.

2. Hone Channels: The hone channel upgrades the image's clarity, making the edges and points of interest indeed more exact.

- Unsharp Cover: The current channel upgrades the picture by expanding differentiates with the edge, making the picture more straightforward. Keen Hone gives modern controls to decrease commotion amid honing, which can be encouraged controlled over the honing framework.

• Shake lessening helps decrease vagary caused by camera shingle, especially in pictures that are inadvertently foggy due to movement.

3. Misshape Channels: Distortion filters are utilized to fictitiously change, pivot, or modify your picture utilizing inventive strategies to include stylish request or to mimic reasonable moves.

- Spheris the picture so that it wraps around a circle, valuable for creating round impacts or an bizarre position.

Twirl the picture to make a whirlpool impact so that the substance appears to spin or contort from the center. Liquefy empowers you to thrust, drag, and distort the picture in a liquid, customizable way ordinarily utilized for modifying but which can moreover include ordinary mutilation.

Artistic Effects and Overlays

In Photoshop Components 2025, you'll be able apply multiple inventive impacts and surfaces to make an exceptional, painterly, or something else finished see to your pictures.

1. Aesthetic Impacts: Oil paints permit you to convert your picture into a fake oil portray with the plausibility of altering brush points of interest, light, and fashion.

• Watercolor: Changes your picture into a watercolor-style portray with delicate edges and streaming colors. Pencil Outline takes after a hand-drawn pencil outline, allowing you to draw suddenly from a photo.

2. Overlays: Sheathing may be a layer connected to an picture which presents surface something else unaffected by changes the understood in satisfied. These can extend from the dirtiest surface to the bokeh impact or indeed the spill of light, giving your picture an additional dynamic and complex layer.

• How to Apply Overlays:

1. Open your picture and go to Record > Put Inserted to moment an overlay.

2. Position and scale the overlay to cover the picture.

3. Alter the moment darkness and mix mode of the layer (e.g. , Overlay, and Soft Light) so as to make a culminate mix between the sheathing and the picture.

Creating Custom Effects and Filters

Photoshop Components 2025 enables you to create custom effects and filters using the built-in tools and layers, contributing more flexibility and personalization to the editing system.

1. Custom Effects with Layer Styles: You can create your own effects by joining layers in a manner identical to Drop Shadow, Bevel, Emboss, and Glow. The above may be custom-made together with other coordinates for transparency, distance, size, and orientation.

• How to Create Custom Effects:

1. Select the layer to apply the effect to.

2. Go to Layer > Layer Style and choose the effect you want.

3. Adjust the settings to match your desired outcome.

4. Take a trip to Windows > Styles and click on the new Style button.

2. Creating Custom Filters with Smart Filters: Smart Filters enable you to apply a non-destructive filter, which you can edit or remove in the following way. You can create a custom filter by stacking and merging several results to produce a unique result using Smart Objects.

• How to Create Custom Filters:

1. Right-click the layer you want to convert to a smart object, then choose Convert to Smart Object.
2. Apply multiple filters from the Filter menu.
3. To fine-tune the final expression, adjust the filter results by masking and merging the Smart Filter.
3. Saving and Applying Custom Presets: Once you have created your custom resonance or filter, you can save it as a preset and apply it to other images. This is particularly helpful if you wish to maintain consistency between different photographs.

• How to Save Presets:

1. After creating your effect or filter, go to the Effects Panel or Filter Gallery.

2. Click the Save button and give your preset a name.

3. Apply it to other images by selecting it from the saved preset list.

CHAPTER SEVEN

Working with Layers and Masks

Introduction to Layers in Photoshop Elements 2025

Layers are one of the most commonly used abstractions in Photoshop. They allow you to create and edit your design in a non-destructive way by putting different aspects of your work on different transparent sheets. The present separation enables flexibility and management in the edit without the possibility of moving other parts of the design.

What Are Layers?

•   Layers can contain images, text, shapes, or effects, stacked one above the other.

The layer at the top of the stack extends beyond that lower layer, creating a composite image.

•   Each layer can be independently edited, moved, resized, or hidden.

Types of Layers

1.   Background Layer: The default layer of an image, typically locked to prevent accidental edits.

2.   Image Layers: Contain photos or other rasterized images.

3.   Adjustment Layers: Allow you to make non-destructive color or tonal corrections.

4.   Text Layers: Created when you add text to your project, remaining editable until rasterized.

5.   Shape Layers: Contain vector shapes created using the shape tools.

6.   Smart Object Layers: Allow for non-destructive editing of images and filters.

7.   Fill Layers: Contain solid colors, gradients, or patterns.

Creating and Managing Layers in Photoshop Elements 2025

1. Making Layers

To form an unused layer:

• From the Layers Board:

1. Open the Layers Board (Easy route: F11 or through Window > Layers).

2. Press the Make a Unused Layer symbol at the foot of the board.

• By means of the Menu: Go to Layer > Unused > Layer and name your layer. To make a transcript, right-click an existing layer and select Copy Layer.

2. Overseeing Layers: Overseeing layers includes organizing, altering, and applying alterations to realize your craved comes about. Reorder layers by dragging layers up or down within the Layers Board to alter their stacking course of action.

Rename layer: Double-click the layer title within the Layers Board, enter a modern title, and press Enter. To stow away or show a layer, press the eye symbol another to it.

To keep the layers associated whereas traveling or changing them, you'll be able relate layers by selecting distinctive layers and snapping the layer symbol. To avoid coincidental changes, use the Bolt symbol within the Layers Board. The choices are bolt state, perceivability, or all alters.

Bunch layer: Select a distinctive layer, at that point imperativeness Ctrl+G (or Command+G on Mac) to gather them together. Cohorts are making a difference to form a complex undertaking.

3. Utilizing Layer Covers: Layer covers let you hide parts of a layer without for all time erasing them: 1. Select a layer and tap the Include Layer Cover symbol within the Layers Board.

2. Utilize a brush to paint dark (to conceal), white (to uncover), or dark (to somewhat uncover).

4. Applying Mixing Modes: Mixing modes control how a layer interatomic with layers underneath it: Select a layer, and from the Blending Mode dropdown within the Layers Board, select Increase, Screen, or Overlay to make more than one result.

5. Erasing Layers

To erase a layer:

• Right-click the layer within the Layers Board and select Erase Layer.

• On the other hand, drag the layer to the Trash Can Symbol in the Layers Board.

Using Layer Masks in Photoshop Elements 2025

Apply a layer style

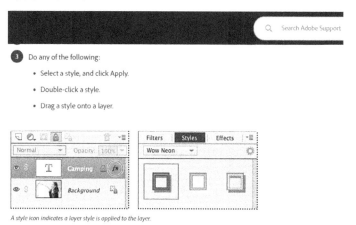

A style icon indicates a layer style is applied to the layer.

If you don't like the result, press Ctrl+Z (Command + Z in Mac OS) to remove the style, or choose Edit > Undo.

Layer Veils permit you to select the parts of the layer that are obvious, concealed, or somewhat unmistakable but not for all time deleted or something else evacuate all components of the layer.

1. Include a Layer Veil:

- Select the layer you need to mask.
- Within the Layers Board, click on the Include Layer Cover symbol, which may be a rectangle with a circle interior.

2. Paint on the Cover: Utilize the Brush Apparatus with dark, white, or gray to characterize perceivability: Dark covers up ranges of the layer. Alter brush measure, hardness, and murkiness for point by point concealing.

3. Refine the Veil: Utilize instruments like Feathering or the Refine Edge choice to smooth moves on the cover.

Adjustment Layers in Photoshop Elements 2025

You'll be able utilize alteration layers to form non-destructive changes to color, tone, and common appearance of a picture that does not alter its unique layer.

They lie past your moment layer of your picture and shape each layer underneath it, unless your veil avoids it.

2. Levels: Adjust the tonal extend by altering shadows, mid-tones, and highlights.

How to Utilize Alteration Layers

1. Include an Alteration Layer:

Go to Layer > Unused Alteration Layer and select the specified adjustment sort. On the other hand, utilize the Alteration Board or make a modern Alteration Layer symbol within the Layers Board. 2. Adjust the Alteration:

Double-click the alteration layer thumbnail within the Layers Board to open its properties. 3. Restrain the Alteration:

Include a Layer Veil to the alteration layer to apply the impact specifically.

Grouping and Organizing Layers in Photoshop Elements 2025

In arrange to oversee complex operations in Photoshop, the frame layer is irreplaceable. Group and organizational procedures, in specific within the field of plan, contribute to streamlining the work prepare.

1. **Gathering Layers:** The Layer Cohort permits you to join together connected layers into a single booklet,

permitting you to move, alter, and oversee them effectively.

• Making a Layer Gather: It Utilize Ctrl/Cmd for a back-to-back layer or Ctrl/Cmd for a non-consecutive layer within the Layers Board. Right-click and select Bunch Layers or press Ctrl+G (Windows) / Cmd+G (Mac).

• Renaming a Bunch:

Double-click the bunch title within the Layers Board and sort a modern title.

• Ungrouping Layers:

Right-click the gather and select Ungroup Layers or drag layers out of the gather.

2. Organizing Layers: Turn around layer arrange Drag layers or categories up and down within the Layers Board to reorder their stacking arrange. • Color Coding Layers: Right-click a layer or gather and allot a color for speedy recognizable proof. Utilizing expressive names of layers, such as 'header content " or' setting picture ", to rapidly find the precise parameters.

• Collapse communities: Tap the bolt following to a gather to extend or collapse it; keep the Layers Board clean.

Using Layers for Non-Destructive Editing

The non-destructive altering highlights of Photoshop make beyond any doubt that the initial image information remains intaglio so that you just can go back and alter the alters free of nonstop changes.

1. Alteration Layers: Alteration layers are a key device for non-destructive altering:

• Make tonal or color alterations without changing the base layer.

• Utilize veils to apply changes specifically.

2. Layer Covers: Layer covers stow away or uncover parts of a layer without erasing substance:

• Paint with dark, white, or gray to control perceivability.

• Combine with alteration layers to apply impacts specifically.

3. Keen Objects: In spite of the fact that Photoshop

angles offer assistance less Savvy Objects have compared to Photoshop, change over layer to Savvy Objects punishments.

• Resizing, turning, and changing without losing quality.

• Applying channels non-destructively.

4. Utilizing Mix Modes: Mix modes alter how layers connected with one another:

• Non-destructive mixing permits you to test with imaginative impacts without for all time combining layers.

5. Clipping Veils: The clipping cover is utilized to align one layer with the shape or perceivability of the another one.

• Valuable for applying surfaces, designs, or alterations to particular parts of an picture.

CHAPTER EIGHT

Photo Merging and Panoramas

Creating Panoramas in Photoshop Elements 2025

Making a see includes joining together diverse photos to create a single fisheye picture. Viewpoints of Photoshop's Photomerge instrument rearrange this procedure.

Steps to Form a Scene:

1. Get to the Photomerge Device:

Go to Record > Photomerge > Display.

2. Select Photographs: Browsing and selecting pictures for Exist sew. For the finest conceivable result, guarantee that the photo contains cover zones.

3. Adjust and Consolidate:

- The instrument will adjust and mix the photographs naturally.
- Alter settings like Auto Format, Viewpoint, or Round and hollow Projection to optimize arrangement.

4. Fine-Tune the Scene: Utilize apparatuses to edit edges or fill crevices with the Content-Aware Fill choice.

Photomerge Apparatus Highlights
1. Photomerge Confront:

Blend facial highlights from a few photos into one idealize picture. For occurrence, select an elective expression from a bunch of pictures.

2. Photomerge Bunch Shot: Combining components from diverse photos to create the finest group photo, ensuring the most excellent appearance of the complete subject.

3. Photomerge Scene Cleaner: Expel undesirable components, e.g. , people may too protest) to a scene by blending a few photos that don't contain any diversion.

Sewing Numerous Photographs
Photoshop Elements' Display Highlight employments progressed sewing calculations:

• Consequently alters for presentation and focal point twisting.

• Adjusts covering areas for consistent moves.

• Incorporates manual refinement alternatives for exact control.

CHAPTER NINE

Using Photoshop Elements for Graphics and Design

Creating Collages and Layouts in Photoshop Elements 2025

Photoshop components make it simple to make eye-catching collages and formats for numerous purposes, such as photo collections, welcoming card diversions, or, on the other hand, social organizing locales.

1. Include Photographs:

Drag and drop photographs from the Organizer or your computer into the format.

2. Customize the Format:

Alter picture situation, turn, resize, or trim pictures inside the format spaces.

3. Include Photographs:

Consequence pictures by dragging them into the canvas or utilizing Record > Put.

Resize and organize the photographs utilizing the Move Device.

4. Plan the Format:

Utilize Direct Lines or the Network (flip with See > Framework) for exact arrangement.

Make a intermediary shape by applying a shapemaker, at that point utilize Nip Veils to connect them with pictures.

5. Improve the Plan:

Include borders, shadows, or impacts utilizing the Layers Board.

• Layer Covers: Mix photographs consistently or make custom shapes.

• Alteration Layers: Fine-tune the presentation or color of person pictures. Sparing and Sharing Your Collage 1. Save Your Venture: o Spare as a PSD record to protect layers for future alters.

Adding Frames and Borders in Photoshop Elements 2025

1. Including Pre-designed Outlines

• Go to Impacts Board > Outlines.

• Select a outline fashion and drag it onto the picture.

• Resize or reposition the outline on the off chance that required.

2. Making Custom Borders

• Manual Strategy:

  • Utilize the Rectangular Marquee Device to form a determination around your picture.

  • Go to Alter > Stroke (Layout) Choice and indicate the width, color, and area of the boundary line.

• Layer Styles: Include a stroke impact to a layer through Layer > Layer Fashion > Fashion Settings.

Applying Designs and Slopes in Photoshop Components 2025

1. Applying Designs

• Select the Paint Bucket Apparatus and select Design Fill from the choices bar.

• Open the Design Picker to choose from preloaded or custom designs.

• Apply the design to your layer or determination.
2. Applying Slopes

• Utilize the Angle Apparatus from the toolbar.
• Select a angle fashion from the alternatives bar (e.g., Direct, Spiral).

• Tap and drag over the canvas to apply the slope.

Working with Shapes and Custom Graphics in Photoshop Elements 2025

1. Adding Shapes

- Use the **Shape Tool** to add basic geometric or custom shapes.

- Choose shape styles, fill colors, and stroke settings from the options bar.

2. Custom Graphics

- Import graphics by dragging files onto the canvas or use built-in graphics from the **Graphics Panel**.
- Customize by resizing, rotating, or applying effects.

CHAPTER TEN

Saving and Exporting Options

Saving for Web and Print in Photoshop Elements 2025

When you are ready to save your project or photograph for a different purpose (web or print), Photoshop Factors 2025 provides a variety of tools to ensure that your images are optimized for their intended use.

1. File Formats: JPEG is the most commonly used format for web photos, scheduled to have a symmetrical relation between file sizes and standard sizes.

2. Steps: Navigate to Folder > Export and select the correct file format (JPEG, PNG, or GIF). It adjust the caliber context for JPEG by decreasing the quality slider to a low percentage to decrease file size for fast web pages loading. File Formats: TIFF: An excellent format for printing that maintains image quality.

JPEG can also be used for printing, but to keep the highest resolution, make sure the standard is set to

100%.

2. Actions: Select the preferred print file format by going to File > Save As.

2. Activities:

Exporting in Different File Formats

Photoshop permits you to choose a record fashion concurring to your needs when sending out pictures then again. Common Send out Designs: JPEG is broadly utilized for web and print applications, guaranteeing great consistency between record measure and picture quality.

3. Alter quality, determination, and measurements agreeing to your needs. Optimizing Record Sizes Maximizing pictures is critical for quicker stack times on beat of a web location or decreasing capacity space without relinquishing as well much standard. 1. Resize Images: Decrease the picture measurements utilizing the Picture Measure discourse (Picture > Resize > Picture Estimate). 2. Alter Quality Settings: In arrange to decrease record measure, within the discourse "Spare for Web,"

reduce the substance within the JPEG record. For PNG, alter compression settings for a littler record estimate without critical misfortune of quality.

3. Utilize the Trade As Exchange: The Send out As discourse permits you to control record measure by selecting the fitting introduction (JPEG with a comparing quality, PNG with optimized compression, etc.

2. Customize the Slideshow: Include moves, music, and captions utilizing the accessible apparatuses.

3. Trade: It spares the slideshow as a video record.

CHAPTER ELEVEN

Troubleshooting and FAQs for Photoshop Elements 2025

There are a few common issues, mistake messages, and execution counsel related to Photoshop components 2025, alongside habitually inquired questions to assist distinguish common deterrents.

Common Issues and Fixes

1. Moderate Execution or Solidifying: Since the components of Photoshop may moderate down if the system necessities are not met, or in case the disk space accessible adjacent isn't adequate. Settle:

• Guarantee your computer meets the least framework necessities (Slam, GPU, etc.).

• Clear transitory records or cache by reaching to Alter > Cleanse > All.

• Near superfluous programs to free up framework assets.

2. Lost Records or Organizers

Cause:

Files or envelopes may be misplaced after a framework upgrade or program crash.

Settle:

• Modify the Organizer database by aiming to Record > Oversee Catalogs and selecting Modify.

• Utilize the Record > Open Later include to rapidly get to later records.

3. Adulterated or Blocked off Crude Records

Cause:

Crude records may be debased or not congruous with the current adaptation.

Settle:

• Guarantee that your camera's Crude organize is bolstered by the computer program.

• Upgrade Photoshop Components to the most recent form to incorporate unused Crude record back. Change over Crude record to a consistent arrange, e.g. , TIFF or JPEG employing a third party converter on the off chance that required.

Error Messages and Solutions

1. "Not Sufficient Slam" Mistake: Typically due to the huge record measure or, then again, a parcel of covered up applications.

Arrangement:

• Near superfluous programs or increment the virtual memory in your framework settings. Endeavor to alter a littler parcel of the picture another to a span, something else diminish the determination of your extend.

2. "Record Cannot Be Opened" Blunder

Cause:

This may happen in case the record is undermined or in an unsupported arrange.

Arrangement:

• Check in the event that the record is consistent with Photoshop Components (e.g., JPEG, PNG, TIFF). Endeavor to open the record in a diverse picture editor to see in case it's harmed. accepting this, and endeavoring to recuperate the archive employing a information recuperation program.

3. "Incapable to Spare" Mistake

Cause:
A full disk or compose consents blunder can anticipate sparing records.

Arrangement:
• Guarantee there's sufficient disk space for sparing the record.
• Check your file's goal envelope for compose authorizations and modify them in the event that fundamental.
• Attempt sparing the record with a diverse title or in a diverse area.

Tips for Progressing Execution

1. Increment Smash Assignment: Expecting you're dynamic nearby a huge record, increment the allocated memory within the choices setting to move forward

your execution. Take a trip to alter, taste, performance, and alter the Slam utilization.

2. Optimize Record Estimate: It diminishes resolution and record estimate for pictures that don't require thymine for way better execution. Utilize picture > Resize to alter the estimate. 3. Cripple Auto-Save: Turn off auto-saving in the event that it moderates down your work stream. You'll be able include this to the Alter > Choices > Organizer Taking care of segment.

4. Overhaul Program Frequently: Guarantee that the angles of Photoshop are overhauled for the most recent form so that they can advantage from bug fixes and execution changes.

Frequently Asked Questions (FAQs)

1. How Do I Convert My Photos to Black and White?

Using the Convert trait, subordinate to Grayscale, you may use the Convert trait to enhance the Black and

White. Alternately, use an adjustment layer for additional control over color consistency and tone.

2. How Do I Use Camera RAW to Edit My Photos?

When you import a RAW file, it will spontaneously open in the Camera RAW Editor, where you can adjust exposure, white balance, sharpness, etc.

3. How Can I Share My Projects Directly on Social Media?

Go to Folder > Share and select an online network platform. To post directly from your software, you need to log in to your digital media explanation within the limitations of Photoshop.

4. How Do I Recover a Lost Photo or Project?

Using the AutoSave or Recovery option under Edit > Choices > File Handling to automatically support a document. If the project is lost, check the Recent Files section or use a data recovery software that provides a crucial feature.

CHAPTER TWELVE

Appendix

Keyboard Shortcuts

It's a great way to accelerate your work in Photoshop by using a keyboard shortcut. For simultaneous Windows and macOS users, here are some of the most useful shortcuts.

General Shortcuts

- Ctrl + N (Windows) / Cmd + N (Mac): Create a new document
- Ctrl + O (Windows) / Cmd + O (Mac): Open an existing file
- Ctrl + S (Windows) / Cmd + S (Mac): Save the current document
- Ctrl + Z (Windows) / Cmd + Z (Mac): Undo the last action

Ctrl + Change + Z (Windows), Cmd + Transition + Z (Mac) Remix the unfinished action.

Navigation Shortcuts

- Ctrl + + (Windows) / Cmd + + (Mac): Zoom in
- Ctrl + - (Windows) / Cmd + - (Mac): Zoom out

- Spacebar: Activate the Hand Tool (for moving around the workspace)

Layer Shortcuts

Ctrl + Change + N (Windows) / Cmd + Change + N (Mac) Create a new layer.

- Ctrl + J (Windows) / Cmd + J (Mac): Duplicate the selected layer

- Ctrl + E (Windows) / Cmd + E (Mac): Merge selected layers

Tool Shortcuts

- V: Move Tool

- M: Marquee Tool

- B: Brush Tool

- S: Clone Stamp Tool

- T: Text Tool

Glossary of Terms

Here's a list of key terms and concepts to help you navigate Photoshop Elements:

Adjustment Layer: A non-destructive layer accustomed to adjusting brightness or contrast which does not change the original image directly.

Clone Stamp: A device that allows you to duplicate parts of an image by copying pixels from one place to another and painting those that are more than that.

• Layer Mask The concealment tool allows you to alternately expose parts of the layer without destroying it, allowing you to make more flexible edits.

Smart Brush: A tool that uses an unintentional adjustment to highlight areas of an image based on its content, e.g. The skin tone is rather than the sky.

The RAW file decompresses the image file of the electronic camera, including all the information captured by the second detector of the camera, allowing more editing possibilities.

Opacity refers to how transparent a layer is; low opacity makes the layer more transparent, while 100% opacity ensures that the layer is fully transparent.

– Device Presets to recover brushes, implements, or other backgrounds so that you can quickly apply them to your business.